Bomb-Sniffing Dogs

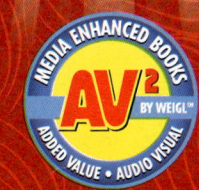

DOGS WITH JOBS

Kara L. Laughlin

AV² provides enriched content that supplements and complements this book. Weigl's AV² books strive to create inspired learning and engage young minds in a total learning experience.

Your AV² Media Enhanced books come alive with...

Audio
Listen to sections of the book read aloud.

Key Words
Study vocabulary, and complete a matching word activity.

Video
Watch informative video clips.

Quizzes
Test your knowledge.

Embedded Weblinks
Gain additional information for research.

Slide Show
View images and captions, and prepare a presentation.

Try This!
Complete activities and hands-on experiments.

...and much, much more!

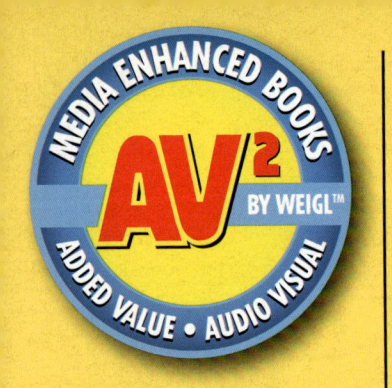

Go to www.av2books.com, and enter this book's unique code.

BOOK CODE

LBM47387

AV² by Weigl brings you media enhanced books that support active learning.

Published by AV² by Weigl
350 5th Avenue, 59th Floor
New York, NY 10118
Website: www.av2books.com

Copyright © 2019 AV² by Weigl
All rights reserved. No part of this publication may be reproduced, stored in a retrieval system, or transmitted in any form or by any means, electronic, mechanical, photocopying, recording, or otherwise, without the prior written permission of the publisher.

Library of Congress Cataloging-in-Publication Data
Names: Laughlin, Kara L., author.
Title: Bomb sniffing dogs / Kara L. Laughlin.
Description: New York, NY : AV2 by Weigl, [2019] | Series: Dogs with jobs | Audience: Age 8-9. | Audience: Grade 4 to 6. | Includes index.
Identifiers: LCCN 2018003644 (print) | LCCN 2018004978 (ebook) | ISBN 9781489677198 (Multi User ebook) | ISBN 9781489677174 (hardcover : alk. paper) | ISBN 9781489677181 (softcover)
Subjects: LCSH: Detector dogs--Juvenile literature. | Working dogs--Juvenile literature. | Explosives--Detection--Juvenile literature.
Classification: LCC SF428.73 (ebook) | LCC SF428.73 .L38 2019 (print) | DDC 636.73--dc23
LC record available at https://lccn.loc.gov/2018003644

Printed in the United States of America in Brainerd, Minnesota
1 2 3 4 5 6 7 8 9 0 22 21 20 19 18

042018
040418

Project Coordinator: Heather Kissock   Art Director: Terry Paulhus

Weigl acknowledges Getty Images, iStock, Newscom, and Alamy as its primary image suppliers for this title. Every reasonable effort has been made to trace ownership and to obtain permission to reprint copyright material. The publishers would be pleased to have any errors or omissions brought to their attention so that they may be corrected in subsequent printings.

First published by The Child's World in 2015

CONTENTS

AV² Book Code 2
Life-Saving Noses 4
The Story of Bomb-Sniffers 7
The Secret Is in the Snout 8
What Do Bomb-Sniffing Dogs Do? 11
Dogs on the Move 12
Logan Black and Diego 14
What Makes a Good Bomb-Sniffer? 17
Training: Sit, Stay, Pay 18
Life as a Bomb-Sniffing Dog 21
Quiz 22
Key Words/Index 23
Log on to www.av2books.com 24

Bomb-Sniffing Dogs   3

Life-Saving Noses

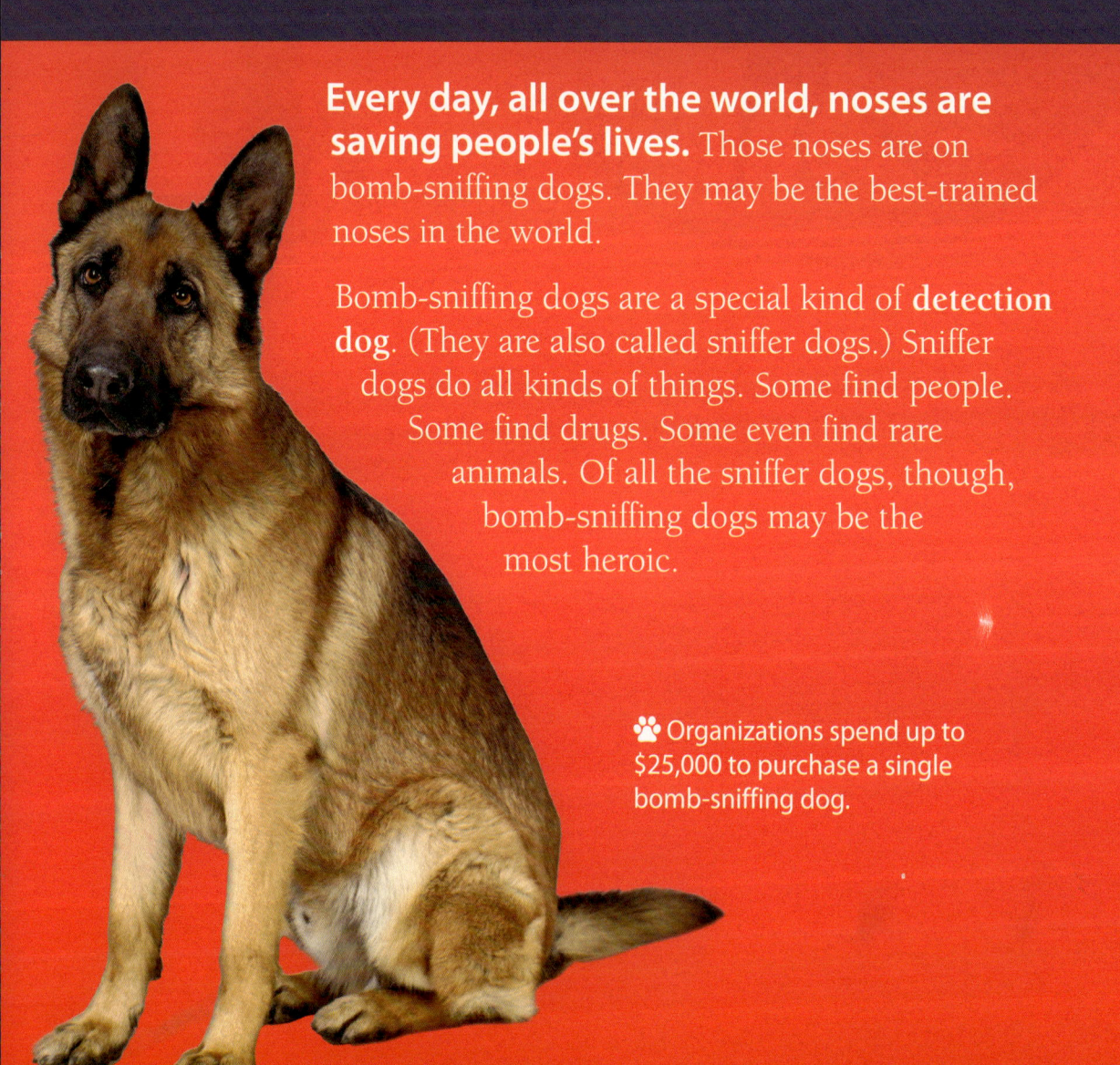

Every day, all over the world, noses are saving people's lives. Those noses are on bomb-sniffing dogs. They may be the best-trained noses in the world.

Bomb-sniffing dogs are a special kind of **detection dog**. (They are also called sniffer dogs.) Sniffer dogs do all kinds of things. Some find people. Some find drugs. Some even find rare animals. Of all the sniffer dogs, though, bomb-sniffing dogs may be the most heroic.

🐾 Organizations spend up to $25,000 to purchase a single bomb-sniffing dog.

🐾 The Transportation Security Administration (TSA) currently employs more than 1,000 teams of bomb-sniffing dogs and their human partners. They work in airports and train stations in the United States.

Bomb-Sniffing Dogs

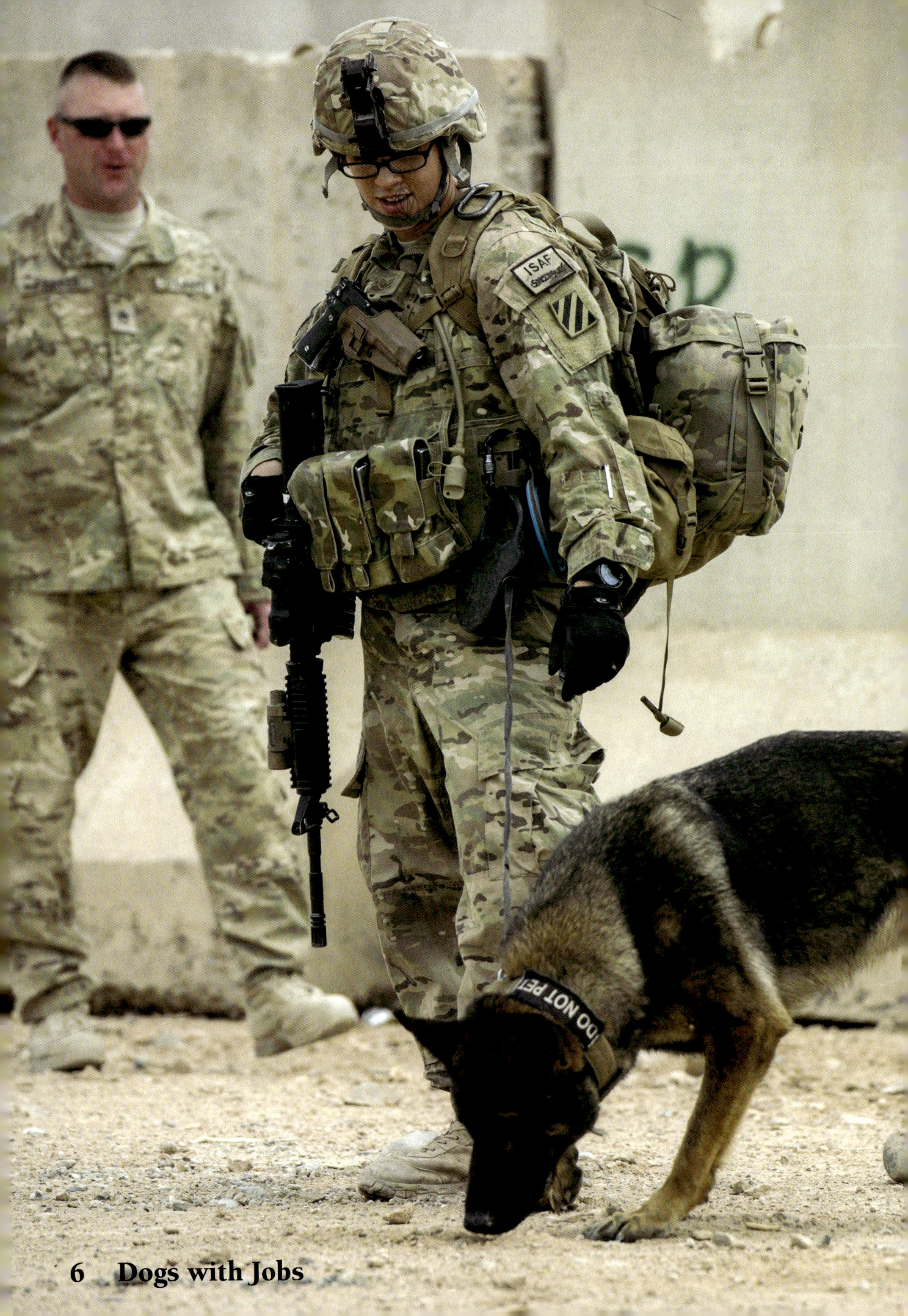
ISAF

The Story of Bomb-Sniffers

The army trained the first U.S. bomb-finding dogs in the 1940s. The dogs were called mine dogs or M-dogs. They were trained to find land mines. Land mines are bombs hidden under the ground. The army could find metal mines with a machine. But some mines were not made of metal. The army couldn't find those mines. Dogs could.

People kept using dogs to find bombs. In 1950, the Los Angeles Police Department put bomb-sniffing dogs on the force. By the 1970s, dogs were finding bombs on airplanes. Today, bomb-sniffing dogs are used all over the world. They help to keep people safe from bombs.

The Secret Is in the Snout

A dog's nose is not like ours. A dog's nose is bigger. It goes all the way from his nostrils to the back of his throat. A dog's nose can suck in more air than a human's. More air means more smells.

Dogs don't breathe like us either. When a dog breathes in, the air splits. Some air goes one way for breathing. Some goes another way for smelling. When he breathes out, air goes out through slits in the sides of his nose. That means dogs can smell while they breathe in and out. This makes them great sniffers.

Bomb-Sniffing Dogs   9

FACTS UNLEASHED

Noses have **odor receptors**. They are like holes for smells to fit into. Dogs have up to 300 million odor receptors, while humans only have about 6 million.

10   Dogs with Jobs

What Do Bomb-Sniffing Dogs Do?

Bomb-sniffing dogs work everywhere. Some work at banks. Some work for sports teams. Others are police dogs. Bomb-sniffing dogs will work any place where a bomb could hurt a lot of people. They might sniff their way through a parade route. They also check places where famous people are going to be. They might check a place where the president is going to speak. Bomb-sniffers also check places where a person says there is a bomb. Sometimes there is a bomb. Most of the time, there is not.

Bomb-Sniffing Dogs 11

Dogs on the Move

Most dogs are trained to find bombs that are in one place. They learn to sniff bags, boxes, and cars. Some trainers have started to teach dogs to find bombs that are on the move. This means they can find people who have a bomb on them. These dogs can smell the bomb's chemicals in the air. Then they follow the smell to the bomb. These dogs are called **Vapor Wake® dogs**.

12   Dogs with Jobs

Bomb-Sniffing Dogs 13

Logan Black and Diego

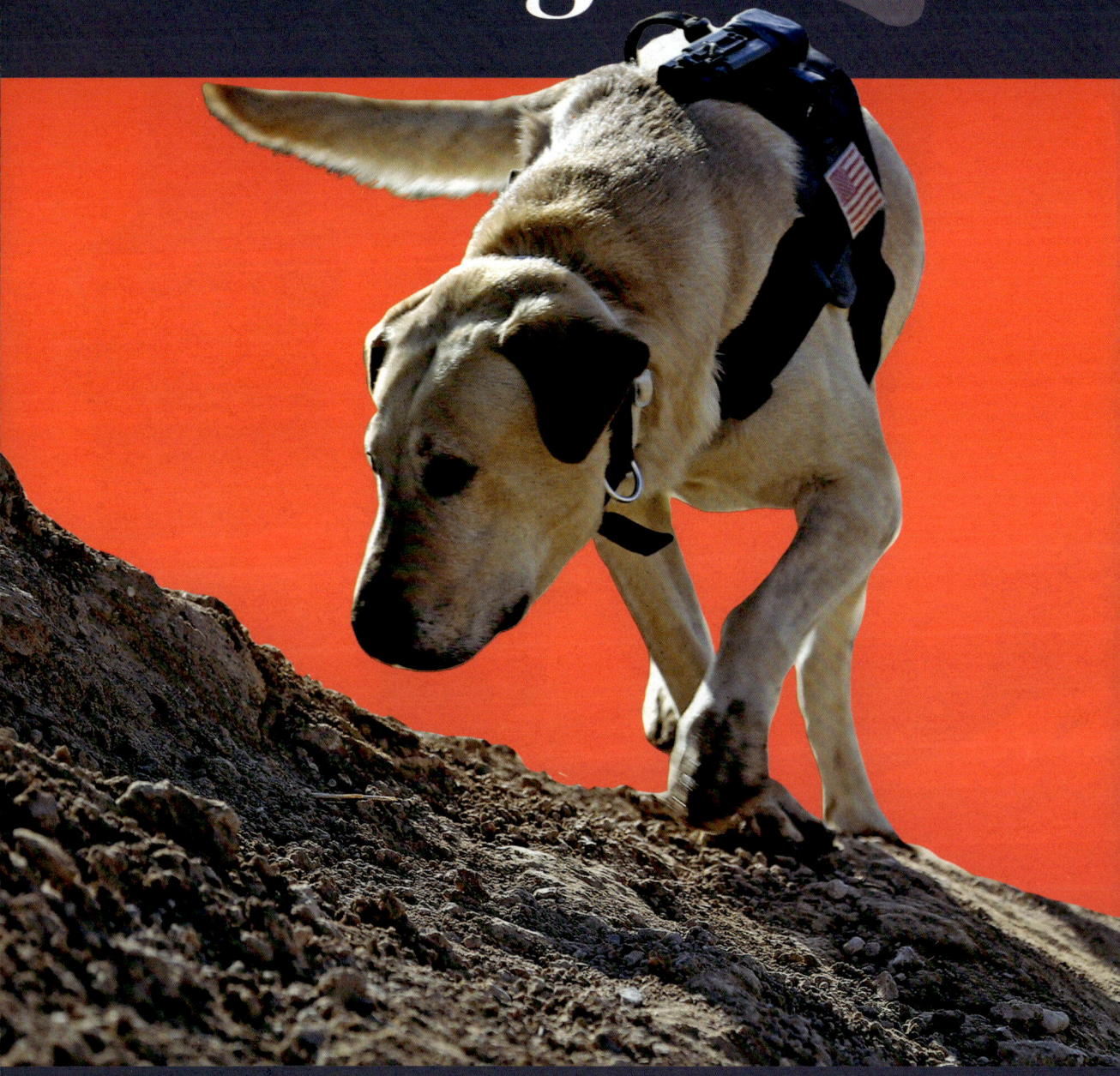

Logan Black and Diego were a bomb-detection team in Iraq. They worked for the U.S. Army. One day while Mr. Black and Diego were on patrol, Diego sat down right next to Mr. Black. Mr. Black knew that Diego had found a bomb. That was strange. The unit had already scanned for bombs. They were supposed to be safe. Mr. Black trusted Diego. He told his unit what Diego had done. Whey they looked, they found two bombs. The bombs were too deep in the ground for metal detectors to find. But they weren't too deep for Diego!

Mr. Black left the army. Diego got a new **handler**. Mr. Black missed Diego. He made a page on Facebook. He asked people to help him find Diego. Mr. Black found Diego, who was now assigned to support the U.S. Air Force. Mr. Black asked the U.S. Air Force to let him adopt Diego. In 2013, Diego and Mr. Black were given an award for their service to the country.

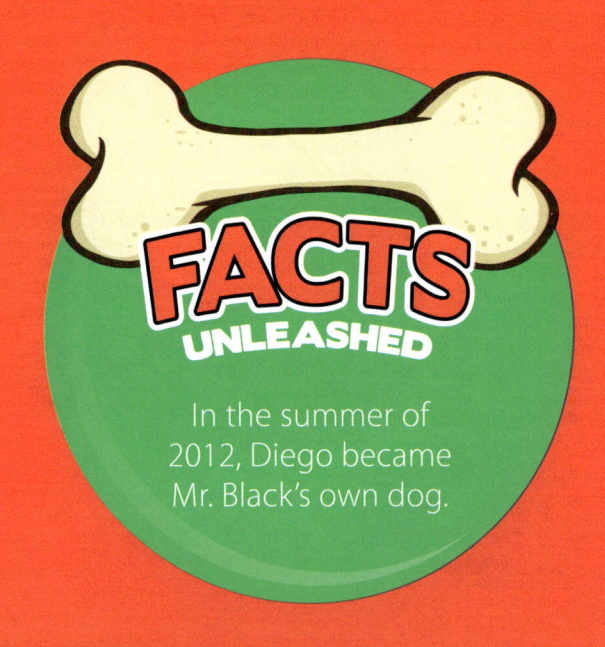

FACTS UNLEASHED

In the summer of 2012, Diego became Mr. Black's own dog.

16   Dogs with Jobs

What Makes a Good Bomb-Sniffer?

Some trainers breed their own sniffer dogs. Others choose adult dogs. They give them a test to see if they will be good at the job. It's not enough to be a good smeller. A bomb-sniffer must also be smart. She should like to play. She must be calm with strangers and do well in crowds. Some breeds that trainers use for bomb-sniffers are Belgian shepherds, Malinois, Labrador retrievers, and Hungarian pointers.

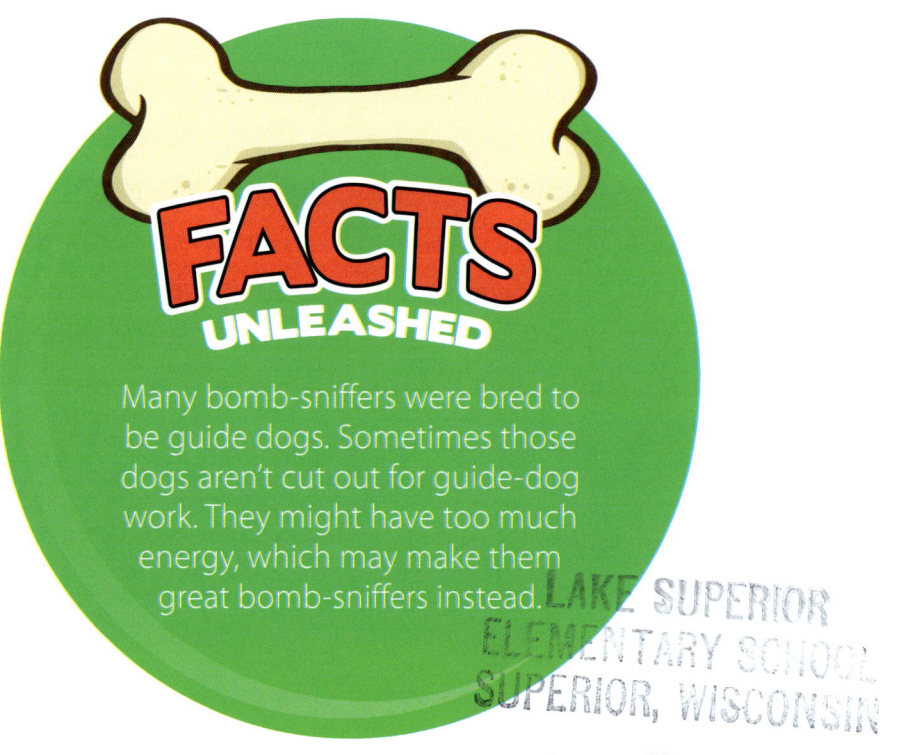

FACTS UNLEASHED

Many bomb-sniffers were bred to be guide dogs. Sometimes those dogs aren't cut out for guide-dog work. They might have too much energy, which may make them great bomb-sniffers instead.

Bomb-Sniffing Dogs 17

Training: Sit, Stay, Pay

Most of the time, dogs start training between one and three years old.

Trainers will hide different kinds of bomb chemicals in a group of cans. The dog learns to sit when he smells one of the chemicals. Then he gets a treat. It could be a little food treat. It could be a toy to tug. Trainers call this kind of training "**Sit, Stay, Pay**." When the dog learns to sit and stay, the trainer pays him back for the good work. Basic training takes about twelve weeks for most dogs.

The dogs might be trained for the place they will work. They learn to sniff the kinds of things that will be on their job. Dogs who will work in airports practice in fake airports. They learn where to sniff on bags and boxes. They even practice on fake planes. When they get to a real airport, they think, "This place has those smells that get me food!"

18   Dogs with Jobs

Bomb-Sniffing Dogs   19

FACTS UNLEASHED

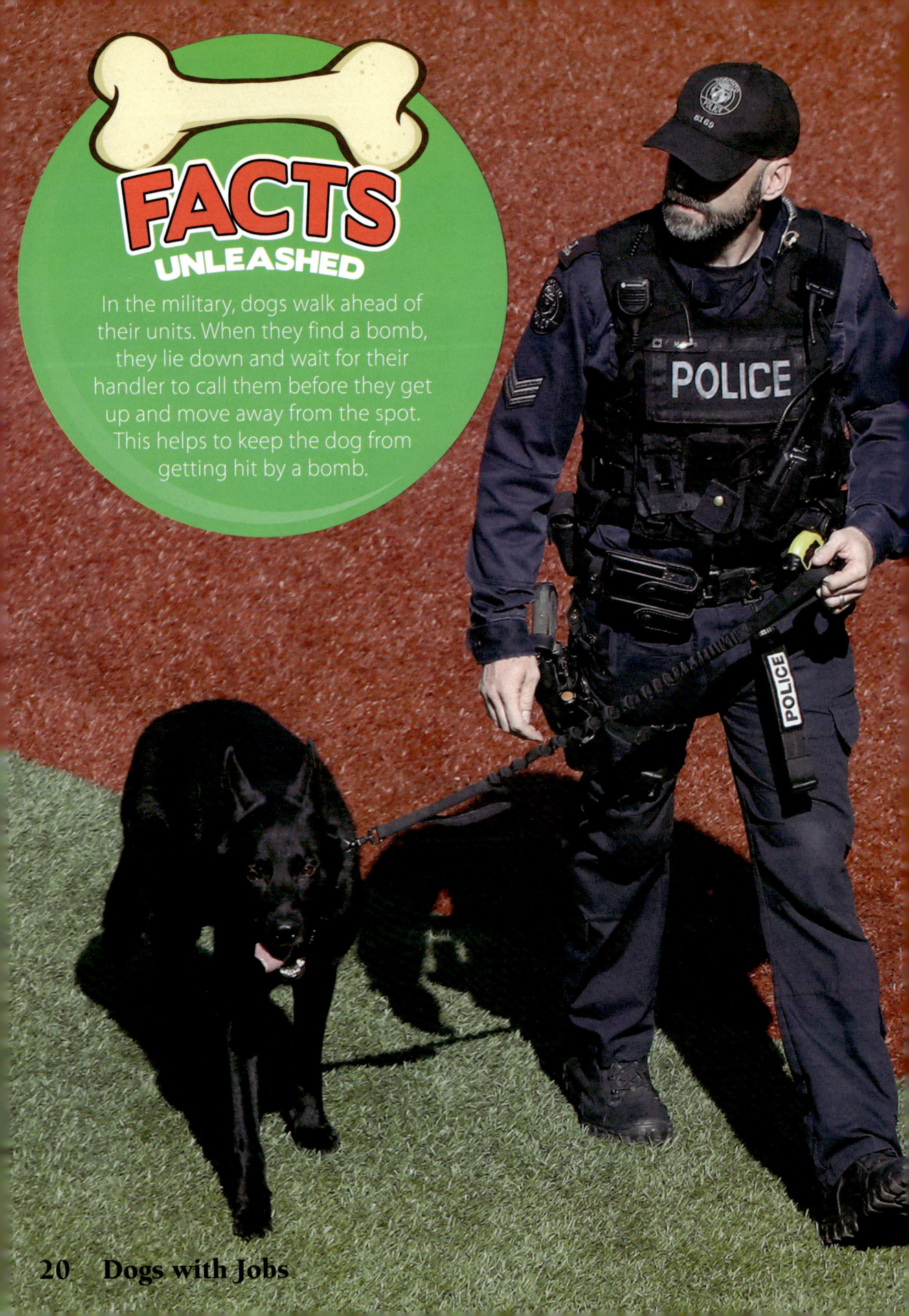

In the military, dogs walk ahead of their units. When they find a bomb, they lie down and wait for their handler to call them before they get up and move away from the spot. This helps to keep the dog from getting hit by a bomb.

20   Dogs with Jobs

Life as a Bomb-Sniffing Dog

Bomb-sniffing dogs work with one person. This is their handler. They work together as a team. Most bomb-sniffing dogs live with their handlers. This helps the dog and handler get to know each other well and build trust.

When a dog goes to work, he sniffs all the places that might have bombs. His handler guides him with a leash. A dog at a school might sniff every locker. A dog working for the police might hunt through a building. Every job is different. All that sniffing makes a dog tired, so the dogs work in teams. When one dog is tired, a new dog gets to work. A good trainer can tell when his dog needs a break.

On most days, dogs don't find bombs. That's good for people, but not so good for the dog. Don't forget, the dog is playing hide and seek. If he doesn't find a bomb, the game isn't fun. He might stop playing. Every day, handlers hide some explosives for the dog to find. That helps the dog remember the smells he needs to find. It also lets him get a treat. Bomb-sniffing dogs practice and take tests for all of their working lives.

Quiz

1 About how long is a bomb-sniffing dog's basic training?

2 When did the U.S. start training bomb-sniffing dogs?

3 What was the name of the person in the army who adopted his bomb-sniffing dog?

4 How old are most dogs when they start bomb-sniffing training?

5 Bomb-sniffing dogs can cost up to what amount each?

6 Can you name one of the four breeds that are commonly used for bomb-sniffers?

7 What city's police department started using bomb-sniffing dogs in the 1950s?

8 What training method teaches dogs that if they sit when they smell a bomb, they'll get a treat?

9 What is the term for the dog's human partner when out on the job?

10 Where do most bomb-sniffing dogs live?

ANSWERS
1 Twelve weeks **2** The 1940s **3** Logan Black **4** One to three years old **5** $25,000 **6** Belgian shepherds, Malinois, Labrador retrievers, and Hungarian pointers **7** Los Angeles **8** Sit, Stay, Pay **9** A handler **10** With their handlers

22 Dogs with Jobs

Key Words

detection dog (dee-TEK-shun DOG): a dog that can find things by smell

handler (HAND-ler): a person who lives and works with a bomb-sniffing dog

odor receptors (OH-dur ree-SEP-turz): the parts of olfactory receptor cells that help detect smells

Sit, Stay, Pay (SIT STAY PAY): the training method that helps a dog learn that he gets a treat when he sits at the location of a bomb scent

Vapor Wake® dogs (VAY-pur WAKE DOGZ): dogs that are trained to follow the smell left by a bomb in the air

Index

Black, Logan 14, 15, 22
breeds 17

detection dog 4
Diego 14, 15, 22

handlers 15, 20, 21, 22
history of 7

Iraq 15

land mines 7
Los Angeles Police Department 7

mine dogs 7

nose 8

odor receptors 10

Sit, Stay, Pay 18, 22
sniffer dogs 4, 17

training 18, 22

U.S. Air Force 15, 22
U.S. Army 7, 15, 22

Vapor Wake® dogs 12

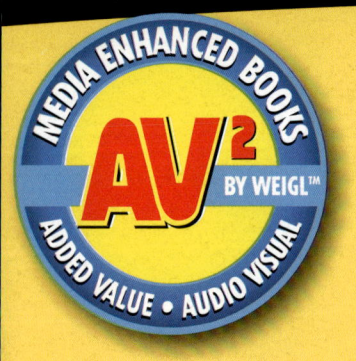

Log on to www.av2books.com

AV² by Weigl brings you media enhanced books that support active learning. Go to www.av2books.com, and enter the special code found on page 2 of this book. You will gain access to enriched and enhanced content that supplements and complements this book. Content includes video, audio, weblinks, quizzes, a slide show, and activities.

AV² Online Navigation

Book Pages
AV² pages directly correspond to pages in the book.

Audio
Listen to sections of the book read aloud.

Video
Watch informative video clips.

Embedded Weblinks
Gain additional information for research.

Key Words
Study vocabulary, and complete a matching word activity.

Quizzes
Test your knowledge.

Slide Show
View images and captions, and prepare a presentation.

Try This!
Complete activities and hands-on experiments.

AV² was built to bridge the gap between print and digital. We encourage you to tell us what you like and what you want to see in the future.

Sign up to be an AV² Ambassador at www.av2books.com/ambassador.

Due to the dynamic nature of the Internet, some of the URLs and activities provided as part of AV² by Weigl may have changed or ceased to exist. AV² by Weigl accepts no responsibility for any such changes. All media enhanced books are regularly monitored to update addresses and sites in a timely manner. Contact AV² by Weigl at 1-866-649-3445 or av2books@weigl.com with any questions, comments, or feedback.

24 Dogs with Jobs